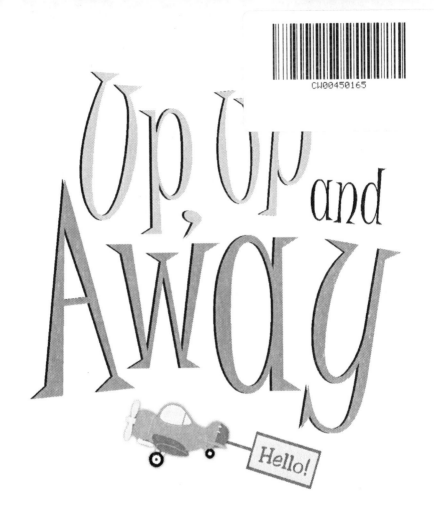

FIFE

Edited by Sarah Andrew

First published in Great Britain in 2000 by
YOUNG WRITERS
Remus House,
Coltsfoot Drive,
Peterborough, PE2 9JX
Telephone (01733) 890066

HB ISBN 0 75432 244 0
SB ISBN 0 75432 245 9

FOREWORD

This year, the Young Writers' Up, Up & Away competition proudly presents a showcase of the best poetic talent from over 70,000 up-and-coming writers nationwide.

Successful in continuing our aim of promoting writing and creativity in children, our regional anthologies give a vivid insight into the thoughts, emotions and experiences of today's younger generation, displaying their inventive writing in its originality.

The thought, effort, imagination and hard work put into each poem impressed us all and again the task of editing proved challenging due to the quality of entries received, but was nevertheless enjoyable. We hope you are as pleased as we are with the final selection and that you continue to enjoy *Up, Up & Away Fife* for many years to come.

CONTENTS

Robert Cail	92
Shaun Masson	93
Johny Hain	94
Rob Drysdale	95
Elizabeth Todd	96
Lissie Kennedy	97
James Foreman	98
Fiona Stratton	99
Amber Ainsworth	100
Joshua Haslam	101

St Agatha's Primary School, Leven

Paul Soutar	102
Craig Ratcliffe	103
Jennifer Dickson	104
Mickeala Lindsay	105
Carla Boyce	106
Craig Bullions	107
Michael Lee	108
Declan Stevens	109

St Columba's Primary School, Cupar

Maria Connelly	110
Claudia Fusaro	111
Vanessa Murray	112
Douglas Williams	113
Stephen MacColl	114
Mark Brown	115
Tarik Kssiaa	116
Kim Blyth	117
Amy McKenzie	118
Amanda Hayes	119
Ella Mackinnon	120
Callum McLaughlin	121
Karis Walker	122
Andrew Stewart	123
Fiona McHardy	124

Judith Keiller	192
Conor Smart	193
Alice Cook	194
Nadine Bruce	195

Tanshall Primary School

Dean Dorans	196
Kirsty McLeod	197
Claire Aitken	198
Kimberley Giles	199
Stacy Baker	200

Tayport Primary School

Allan Mill	201
Lorna Gray	202
Andrew Reid	203
Coral Robertson	204
Paul Martin	205
Laura Redpath	206
Nicola Whatley	207
Laura Towns	208
Bradley Burnett	209
Stacey Mullen	210
Zarra Swan	211
Paula Hughes	212
Ruth Barnett	213
Scott Crosby Reid	214
Rebecca White	215
Kimberley Clark	216
Steven Grogan	217
Shannon Moncur	218
Lauren McGivney	219
Rachel Hutchison	220

Thornton Primary School

Nicola Gourlay	221
Matthew Low	222
Daniel Robinson	223

The Poems

WAR IS SAD

War is sad.
People suffer all night long
People die
Families cry.

War is sad.
Guns and violence
Bodies scattered
Missing people.
The big black battle ended today,
People have joy in their lives, hooray!

Laura Robertson (9)
Aberhill Primary School

METHIL

M ethil is an
E xciting
T own it
H as
I ncredible chip shops and
L ibraries.

Alan Stein (9)
Aberhill Primary School

MY BIRTHDAY

It was my birthday.
With lots and lots of friends.
But when they saw the candles, they tried to blow them out.
When we heard the music, we danced and danced around.
Then it was present time
I got big things and small things.
Then we played some games.
I won one.
Then it was time to go.

Coral Petrie (9)
Aberhill Primary School

BATS

B ats swooping down
A t people
T aking their blood
S caring people.

David Allan (9)
Aberhill Primary School

DANGEROUS MAGIC!

Wizard making
itchy potion
zapping
everything zapping away
real magic
dangerous magic!

Alan McBay (9)
Aberhill Primary School

SEASONS

Spring is great!
Pretend to hibernate
Rabbits and lambs are born
At the crack of dawn
Never-ever open the bin
Gusts of wind get in!
                    Seasons!

Summer is fun
Under the sun
Mothers are preparing picnics
Marmalade and mashed potatoes
Eggs and ice-cream
Rice and raisin sandwiches.
                    Seasons!

Autumn is cool
Under the
Trees,
Undiscovered nests are
Mostly seen
Never safe!
                    Seasons!

Winter is cold
In the snow
Nuts and leaves are buried.
The squirrels search
Each secret store and
Rest in nice warm nests.
                    Seasons!

Jane Robertson (9)
Capshard Primary School

PIGEON

P ecks at feet
I ncredibly stupid
G ets into trouble
E njoys eating stale food
O n top of a roof
N othing it can't eat.

Sean Cameron (9)
Capshard Primary School

MY NAME

J okes
E nergetic
N ame is Jennifer
N ice
I ntelligent
F riendly
E ars pierced
R emembers

A nimals
L ovable
E njoys drives in the countryside
S ensible
S wimming
A dventurous
N aughty, a bit
D rama
R ollerblading
A berdeen is where my cousin lives

S porty
I ce skating
M ountain climb
P olar bears are cute and cuddly
S cotland is where I come from
O n my bike I like to ride
N ice clothes.

Jennifer Alessandra Simpson (9)
Capshard Primary School

SPACE PLACE

Space quite a nice place,
Where you can see,
Stars
And even maybe Mars
And Venus,
What about Uranus
Space quite a nice place.

Sean Smith (9)
Capshard Primary School

CHRISTMAS

C is for Christ child, the first born
H is for the holly we put on our door
R is for the red, red robin
I is for the ice we slide on
S is for the snow we play in
T is for the Christmas tree
M is for a Merry Christmas
A is for the angel
S is for Santa Claus.

Rachel Adams (9)
Capshard Primary School

FOOD FOR THOUGHT

Oh no! My buttons will not fasten.
That means I'll have to do some fasting.
But then again, I could try some healthy eating and
Hopefully there will be no cheating.
No more chocolate, no more fattening snacks
Fizzy drinks and unhealthy convenience packs.
Oh how hard it will be,
But I'm making sure I will be a healthier me!

Nadia Winnick (10)
Capshard Primary School

THE WEDDING

I like going to weddings,
but *not* their endings.
This time, I've got lots of pride
because my mum's the bride.
I'm the bridesmaid, it feels great.
It's going to be a special date.
I like wearing silk.
Granddad wears a kilt.

Rianne Miller (9)
Capshard Primary School

EGYPT

Out in the desert, a pyramid lies
Shining with gold and scraping the skies
Standing strong, although it's old
Holding his pharaoh in solid gold.

Out in the desert an Egyptian writes
The sun goes down for colder nights
As the robbers make a plan
To go and rob a wealthy man.

Out in the desert as many years passed
Howard and his crew came to ask
'Where is the tomb of Tutankhamun?'
'I hope that I find him extremely soon.'

Leah Meharry (11)
Capshard Primary School

EGYPT POEM

Sunny skies and boiling-hot sand,
Tons of desert covers the land,
In the Valley of the Kings there are several tombs,
Some of them even have a couple of rooms.

The River Nile floods every year,
The poor people in Egypt always drank beer,
Egypt always had lots of kings,
Each had some servants and other great things.

Carter found Tutankhamun's death mask,
It took five whole years to complete this task,
Tutankhamun became king when he was a very young boy,
A little thing that made sparks was his favourite toy.

Poor people ate something called dates,
While rich people ate fancy cakes,
Wealthy people drank posh wine,
Day, night and all the time.

There are three pyramids in Giza,
Once you see them they'll definitely please ya,
The Egyptians believed in the afterlife,
Most of the pharaohs had more than one wife.

Lyndsey Neillands (11)
Capshard Primary School

EGYPT POEM

Cairo is full of tourists,
The heat is such a trial,
It has a great museum,
On the east bank of the Nile.

It has lots of massive pyramids,
The capital is Cairo,
It has a lot of beaches,
Just for you and your lilo.

Look at Cairo and Luxor,
They are both very popular,
Just because they are mainly desert,
With the sand they stretch so far.

Steven Ward (11)
Capshard Primary School

EGYPT

Egypt is very hot.
You'll see the camels trot.
Up to the pyramids they go so fast.
I'm going on a journey into the past.

I'm back in the time of Tutankhamun.
People really worshipped him.
With mummies and tombs with so many rooms.
How did Egyptians build them?

Pyramids so high,
Nearly touching the sky.
No lorries or trucks.
People worked on their own.
Carrying big pieces of stone.

I have come to the end and I hope you have
Learned what it was like for the Egyptians.
No modern equipment, things were different,
There is so much history in Egypt.

Michelle Gilmour (11)
Capshard Primary School

THE HUMAN BODY

Our body is such a wonderful thing
Somehow our bodies allow us to sing
We learn to walk and we learn to talk
Our body even deals with shock.

We have our senses, five in all
Which we learn to use when we are small
Our major organs help us to live
Here's a gift that we can give
Our body's such a wonderful thing.

Our body has so many parts
It even has a great big heart
We have our arms, hands and legs
Even a tongue for what is said.

We have veins where our blood flows
And when we blush it makes us go
We have a brain that makes us remember
We have a nose that goes red in December.

Don't forget the love we give
It really wants to make me live
Our body has so many parts
Especially, the great big heart.

Louise Milne (10)
Capshard Primary School

MY TEETH

I can taste
my toothpaste.
It keeps my little teeth clean.
I brush them after breakfast
until they shine and gleam.
My brush is see-through plastic,
it works real hard for me.
Now everyone can see
my teeth sparkle perfectly.
My dentist says I'm a superstar,
no fillings for me today.
Now people travel from near and far
to get a look at me.

Steven Ward (10)
Capshard Primary School

CHOCOLATE

Chocolate is the *best* thing made on Earth.
Hundreds of bars are bought in Perth.
One or two bits are never enough
'Cos I eat and eat until I'm stuffed!
Orange filled ones are just as nice,
Little crumbs are left in a trice.
At Christmas I get tons of it,
Then I think my tummy's gonna split.
Every day I can't live without . . . *Chocolate!*

Janey Crichton (10)
Capshard Primary School

SAFE IS NEVER THE WORD FOR ROADS

Roads are never safe
Over the roads we cross
After the sun is down the danger comes out
Daytime is safer than night.

Safe is never the word for roads
   Adults are upset to
      Find their child in pain.
         Even more upset to find
            Their child dead.
            Year by year in pain to find your child in a grave
            If you don't cry you will be brave
            If you look after your child,
            Your child will stay alive.

Sasha Mackie (10)
Capshard Primary School

A FISHY TALE

I must go down to the harbour today,
To catch some fish in the shaking sea,
I really hope that I catch something
Otherwise I'll starve,
Because I always have fish for my tea.

I must go down to the harbour today,
To catch some fish in the windy sea,
It is pretty noisy
And hard to fish,
With seagulls crying and flying.

I must go down to the harbour today,
To catch some fish in the blue and white sea,
I've got my bait
And my rod ready,
So now I'm ready to go.

I must go down to the harbour today,
To catch some fish in the very wild sea,
I have driven down to the harbour
In my car,
So now I'm ready to fish.

I must go down to the harbour today,
To catch some fish in the choppy sea,
I've cast my rod,
So now I must wait
To see if I catch anything.

I must go down to the harbour today,
To catch some fish in the North Sea,
Oh! there is a tug on my rod,
Yes! I have caught something at last
So now I can have my tea.

Michael Watson (10)
Capshard Primary School

THE SEA MEETS THE MIST

It was the day of the storm
And the sea was calm.
No mist, no rain, no nothing
But then
The storm
Mist came and hit the sea
It was like an argument
The sea was breaking with waves, roaring with anger
Evil with force and crying with laughter
It was like a song too
The wind and the rain both hit the
   Sea
The seagulls were all over the place
Some were dead
Some were still alive
At night the storm finished
The sea was calmer
Things were wrecked too.

Kristine Shand (10)
Capshard Primary School

BEST FRIENDS

B est friends are for company,
   someone to trust and share your secrets with.
E veryone needs a best friend,
   they can be met in school, nursery or your street.
S omeone who looks out for you at all times is a best friend.
T aking a friend to the pictures or a day out
   can be exciting for you and your friend.

F alling out can be sad but making up is better.
R eal friends are kind and helpful and also trusting people.
I ce-skating and roller-skating is fun for you and your friends.
E ven best friends might have the same likes or dislikes.
N ight times are also enjoyable for your friends.
D iscos are a lot of fun for you and your friends too.
S ome people have more than one best friend, do you?

Melissa Arnott (10)
Capshard Primary School

I'M BETTER THAN YOU

My dad's richer than your dad,
bigger and better too.
He has a red ferrari,
I'm much better than you!

My mum's tidier than your mum
a lot more diamonds too.
She has her own swimming pool,
I'm much better than you!

We have our private jet
we own Florida too.
We have our own theatre,
I'm much better than you.

My uncle is Chris Tarrant
he works on TV too.
My sister is Britney Spears,
I'm much better than you.

My aunty is Shania Twain
my cousin is popular too.
They both have a Mercedes,
I'm much better than you.

I have my own shopping mall
I have a palace too.
I got the award of Hard Worker of the Year
I'm much better than you!

Nicola Norcross (10)
Capshard Primary School

TRAVEL

Travelling round the world we go
Rattling wheels and trains going by.
Arriving at the stations that are very noisy
Very many people seem to travel the world.
Everyone travels by train, bus, car, aeroplane, or ship
Lots of people travel abroad and some stay here.

Sarah Hunter (10)
Capshard Primary School

MY FAMILY

My family is ever so strange
My brother is a pain
I mean he's insane
He picks his nose
But doesn't even cut his toes
My brother is a pain.

My sister is mad
I mean she's mad about this lad
He's as tall as a wall
He's as skinny as a pin
And he doesn't even have a bin.

My parents are dumb
My mum has a big bum
My dad thinks he's bold
But really he's just old.

My grandma has a full grown moustache
But grandpa doesn't even have a tache
Sometimes I get them mixed round
Then they hit me and I fall on the ground.

Are your family so weird?
Does your mummy have a beard?
Does your dad wear a skirt?
Does your brother always flirt?
Does your sister like this lad?
Is your family ever this mad?

Leela Smith (10)
Capshard Primary School

MY BIRTHDAY

My birthday was coming up soon
And my mum was in stress again
Because I wanted for my birthday
A remote controlled plane
Remote-controlled car
Playstation games
Computer games
Airfix models
Engineering kit
Drawing sets
Sky Digital
Will she get it all in time?
Maybe!

David Robertson (10)
Capshard Primary School

LAURA

L aura's
A lways caring
U nbelievable
R ight
A nd wrong

G oing to
R ead
A nd
N ever stop
T aking care of people

Laura Grant (9)
Capshard Primary School

CLAIRE IS GREAT

C   laire is clever
L   oving
A   is for her ability
I   mportant
R   ight
E   xciting

I   ncredible
S   pecial

G   reat
R   ubbish at Maths
E   njoys watching TV
A   lways wanting to help
T   errible at work, so don't ask.

Claire Keith (9)
Capshard Primary School

ME

A shley
S arcastic
H ilarious
L oving
E xciting
Y ear 2000

B orn in
A ugust
R ight-handed
K ind
E ntertaining and
R ubbish at Maths.

Ashley Barker (9)
Capshard Primary School

MY POEM

N   is for a noisy girl
I   is for an intellectual girl
C   is for a caring person
O   is for an odd little girl
L   is for a loving girl
A   is for an alert person.

P   is for her last name Patrick
A   is for an accurate girl
T   is for a thankful girl
R   is for a girl who likes the radio
I   like ice cream
C   laire is my friend
K   een on everything.

Nicola Patrick (9)
Capshard Primary School

ROAD SAFETY

R oads can be dangerous
O nly the Green Cross Code will save your life
A nd wear a helmet when you're on your bike
D on't run across the road.

S afety is very important to all of us
A lways stop before crossing the road
F ast cars, slow cars, you could get hurt
E ven if it is light, still wear a helmet
T raffic can be very fast, so don't run across the road
Y our life depends on the Green Cross Code.

Jennifer Balfour (11)
Capshard Primary School

WINTER

Above the houses, chimneys smoke
Under the leaves the red robin sleeps.
In the houses fires crackle
On the hill frosty snowmen stand.
Above the houses snow falls
Outside it is bitter cold.

Rachel Ferguson (10)
Coaltown Of Balgonie Primary School

WINTER

In the trees the owl sleeps.
Over the house the snowballs fly.
Beside the cars the children play.
On the windowpane the icicles dangle.
In the houses the flames flicker.
And in their bed the children sleep.

Nicola Gordon (10)
Coaltown Of Balgonie Primary School

WINTER

In my bed I start to quiver.
In the leaves happy hedgehogs hibernate.
In the sky robins fly very high.
Below the snow I don't know where to go.
Across the lane there's
a white windowpane.
In the snow
the snowmen sing.
On the tree the icicles dangle.
In the street
the snow gets
in my feet.

Christopher Penman (10)
Coaltown Of Balgonie Primary School

WINTER DAYS

Scarves,
gloves
all
keep warm.
Snowman
made with
snow-white snow.
Crackling fires.
Keep warm.

Victoria Johnson (9)
Coaltown Of Balgonie Primary School

WINTER

Along the gutter the icicles sparkle.
Beside the window the snowman spies.
Outside the house, bitter winds bite.
Inside the lounge the blazing fire burns.
On the hedge a red robin sings.
Among the leaves animals sleep.
In the kitchen a turkey grills.
Outside the house all is white.
On the roof chimneys smoke.
In the house all is calm.

Kirsty McKean (10)
Coaltown Of Balgonie Primary School

WINTER

Over our heads the chimney smokes.
Up on the wall the little robin bobs.
In the houses the fires are warm.
On the path snowflakes fall.
In the warmth people sleep.
Outside my house a snowman shivers.
In the house I am sleeping in the warm bed.
Outside everybody is freezing like snow.

Stephanie Stewart (9)
Coaltown Of Balgonie Primary School

WINTER

Up in the tree the robins sing.
Below the snow the wet ground lies.
In the garden the snowman melts.
Between the houses the snowflakes fall.
Out the chimneys the smoke floats.
In the houses the fires crackle.

Dean Ritchie (9)
Coaltown Of Balgonie Primary School

WINTER

In the garden a snowman stands.
On the wall a shivering robin sings.
On the old oak icicles dangle.
In the winter I get a runny nose.
Among the crispy snow the hedgehog sleeps.
Through the gate you slip and slide.
In the park a snow fight was due.
In front of me a fire crackles.
Down the lane lies crunchy snow.
Under the tree a squirrel hides.
Along a path into my gate I get some cocoa for me.
Out the gate your silent dreams come true.

Dionne Wallace (9)
Coaltown Of Balgonie Primary School

WINTER

Under the tree the leaves lay low.
In the park the snow stays still.
Outside the house the man chops trees.
Over the house the robin sits.
Up the hill lies lots of snow.
Out jump the children playing with snow.
Then comes spring, snow's all gone.

Karl Zarins (10)
Coaltown Of Balgonie Primary School

WINTER

In the field the snow falls heavily.
Over the hill the children play.
In the house the fire crackles.
Above the houses the chimneys smoke.
Beside the wall the crunching leaves lie.
Under the bridge the small stream freezes.
In the water the winter secret lies.

Jane Campbell (9)
Coaltown Of Balgonie Primary School

WINTER

In the houses the fires crackle.
In the leaves the hedgehogs hide.
Under the snow the grass grows.
In the garden the robins sing.
On the houses icicles drop.
Out in the garden snowmen quiver.
On the rooftops snow lies thick.

Adam Macey (10)
Coaltown Of Balgonie Primary School

WINTER WONDERLAND

In the house a fire is switched on.
Under the snow the cold ground hides.
Up above the dove the clouds are white.
Down beneath the snow the hedgehog sleeps.
Between the trees, above the bush, lies lots of snow.
Beside the bush are nuts from squirrels who ate them in the spring.

Lewis Wake (9)
Coaltown Of Balgonie Primary School

ODE TAE A ROAST CHICKEN

Yer gravy so tasty,
Yer smell so braw,
A' this because of Maw.

You taste like heaven,
You look just richt,
A wish I could hae you ev'ry nicht.

After I've finished I feel so fu'
Oh, Roast Chicken I love you!

Scott Wood (11)
Collydean Primary School

ODE TO A CHICKEN

Ye look like a fitba wi a heid an' wings,
Ye taste sae guid yer fit for kings,
Yer smell wafts up ma nostrils, it never ceases,
We sit doon tae eat like quiet wee meeces.

Yer richt broon skin wi gravy an a';
Yer a favourite in the family especially wi paw,
Yer mentioned tae me, ma tongue starts licken,
A never could live withoot yon *chicken!*

Catherine Farrell (11)
Collydean Primary School

BIRD

I take off into the cloudy sky,
Where I glide to the sun,
I raise my wings to the air,
Where I fly like a kite in the light,
A tear, a frown, I'm always here.
I hover through the sky,
To go far upon the sun
And to hurry back home,
To feed my young.
When I sit down in my nest,
I keep my eggs warm,
They hatch, crackle like crisps,
Twitter and tweet,
They start to eat very little,
And day by day,
They flourish to fly,
Up through the mountains,
Up through the rainbow,
And when the winter,
Comes at last,
They fly south,
Far, far away,
Looking for better weather.

Samantha Skelly (11)
Collydean Primary School

FIREWORK

Up, up
The firework goes up into the sky
The colours look so beautiful
In the sky everyone stands and looks at the sky
The sky is lovely and blue
It makes lots of noises
Just like me
It makes me smile and cheer.

Michelle Johnstone (10)
Collydean Primary School

TO A PIZZA

A big, round pizza base
I like you.
Just add cheese and tomatoes
Then you'll be ready to go.
Put you in the oven
For a few minutes
At last it's ready.
Careful now, I don't want to drop it,
If I do it'll be covered in dirt.
I'll put it on a plate
And add a bit of pepper
And you'll never be better.

Stephen McLachlan (11)
Collydean Primary School

ROCKET RUMBLE

Oh rocket way up in the clouds
You gather so many crowds
Up with the Martians
How good it must be
Oh rocket! Oh rocket!
What can you see?

I can see the moon just above me
Oh rocket! It looks so small to me
I can see the stars and Mars
Oh rocket! All I can see is cars, not even a star.

Oh rocket! Will you come down,
I have got a big, huge frown
OK but not yet
I have just caught up with a big, huge jet.

Vicki Rutherford (10)
Collydean Primary School

SPACE MAN

I am a space man.
I have a rocket.
I go into space all the time.
I fly past the moon, Mars and Jupiter.
I go to Pluto and on the way back
I stop at Venus.
I see a blue alien
With six eyes and ten arms.
I have a rocket with three blast jets,
It is white and very big.
I see a UFO with a green laser.
I land in the sea when I come back,
I say 'Houston we are back safe, over.'

Callum Stewart (10)
Collydean Primary School

TO A PIZZA

Coming home it cannot be,
Pizza on the oven tray,
Cooking there, looking tasty,
Loads of cheese just melting there.
Put some more on,
It'll taste better,
Turn it off,
Or it'll get burnt!
Take it out,
It may get cold,
Eat it now,
Nice and crispy.

Michael Leiper (10)
Collydean Primary School

SHARK

I am a shark swimming in the sea, looking for my tea.
Swimming low and swimming fast, looking very vast.
Surrounded by sand, weeds and rocks, that's what I can see
If I wasn't a shark, there's nothing I would rather be.
I come across a shoal of fish, I eat them all in one,
They taste very good, warm and yummy
But still not enough to fill my tummy.
I swim along to find some more,
I eat some plankton as they soar
Through the water and into my mouth!
They tasted better than the others.
I swim very near to a small, brick castle
Outside it's golden, mouldy walls glitter in the sunlight.
More sharks I see swim up to me
We chase each other as we play.
Swimming fast through seaweed and plants
Some more sharks join in our play.
This has been a wonderful day
Life is great being a shark
I'll swim and play again tomorrow.

Robert Brady (11)
Collydean Primary School

LIKE A ROCKET

It takes off with a blast of light,
Soaring up with all its flight.
Its gigantic boosters
Like two large joosters.
It jets off into space,
Racing past the stars,
Seeing other rockets,
There was a race,
There was a dinner,
I thought it was a winner!

Jamie Meacher (11)
Collydean Primary School

ODE TO A MACARONI CHEESE

O macaroni cheese a cin eat it te it
Comes oot I ma knees a wis born ti eat it
A love it so much that ma mooth drules
When a think about it or when a see it.

It smells so lush that a cid eat o'dy
And o'night the smell guids me ti where
It is when au scoffed it doon and scoff
A ner en doon an when a come home fe
Scill open the door an when a smell it
Ma mooth waters like mad.

Christopher Cleave (11)
Collydean Primary School

ODE TAE CHEESE

There it is, on the table,
Shining like the sun,
A pick it up and scoff it doon,
Richt into ma tum.

A gang tae the fridge,
And whit do a see,
Another big bit o' cheese for me,
It tastes like heaven.

It mak's me feel like wantin' mair;
It smells like paradise,
It looks so awfy, awfy braw,
I wish the world was cheese.

Michael McKinnon (11)
Collydean Primary School

TO A PIZZA

Oh pizza so great,
A' just canny wait,
For yir brilliant taste o'guidniss,
Wi' cheese and pepperoni,
Yir sure nae auld cronie,
Sometimes yir taste knocks me heedliss.

Yir taste is so good,
I just wish I could,
Scoff ya right doon ma throat,
Tomato and cheese,
Could I have some, please?
No doubt you've certainly got ma vote.

Yir taste is so braw,
It'll never go away,
It'll stay wi me forever,
I luv yir taste,
It'll never go to waste,
Yir taste I'll always remember.

So great is yir taste,
It'll never go to waste,
Yes you really are ma favour,
Gimme some more,
I really adore,
A slice o' yir natural flavour.

Scott Ewen (10)
Collydean Primary School

ODE TO MINCE AND TATTIES

Fae the day you boiled in the pan
Washed fae your dirty shell.

Pit with ain in the pan
And made to tatty mash
Covered with gravy which makes the
Perfect tatty mash.

But you pink worms bubbling in
A pot will soon turn brown,
Which Gran gets at the town.

Pit them both together and I will
Let you find out for yourself
If you get a bad taste
Just add some gravy and there wilny
Be any better taste.

Paul Quigley (11)
Collydean Primary School

ODE TAE PIZZA

I'm a'ways longing for a piece,
Wi' extra ham an' extra cheese.
Am' a'ways askin' me maw,
If I can hae a slice or even two!
The smell o' the braw, bubblin' cheese
But nae pepper 'cause it maks ma sneeze,
When I smell the boilin' hot ham,
It maks me a'ways say 'Thank ye mam!'

The smell o' gorgeous cheese and tomato
Maks a shiver go up ma spine sae
I think to nicht,
I just micht
Hae some pizza fir' ma' tea,
Who loves pizza? Aye that's me,
So I just need tae say
I'll hae a pizza any day!

Karen McIntosh (11)
Collydean Primary School

ODE TAE MINCE AN' TATTIES

Ma' maw makes mince an' tatties,
An' it makes me awflly fatty.
Wi' yer mince an' tatties ya' usually have neeps,
But a' dinnae 'cause they make me weep.

Ma' gran an' maw,
Cook it awflly braw,
But ma' daddy cannae cook it brae
'Cause he cannae cook at aw'.

Ryan McGregor (11)
Collydean Primary School

ONE BIG CLOUD UP IN THE SKY

One big cloud up in the sky
One big cloud saying goodbye
I wonder what it means
I really do
It looks like a bird in the sky
It's fading away I wonder why
Is it me fading away
Or is it my happiness saying goodbye?
It looks like a fish, a very thin fish
I wonder what it means
I really do
Maybe it's me getting thinner
Or is it my happiness getting thinner
It's fading away a little quicker
One little cloud up in the sky
One little cloud saying goodbye
I wonder what it means
I really do.

Eirian Taylor (11)
Creich Primary School

FRIEND

My friend is helpful
My friend is caring
My friend is nice
Even when we are playing.
We go for a walk
We go for a run
We go for a jog
Just for fun.
We eat our sweets
We play with our toys
We like to talk
All about boys.
She walks me home
I say bye, bye
Then I start to cry.

Heather Bissett (11)
Dunino Primary School

HOPE

In the cold, dark war
As the bombed fields lie empty
With the trenches deserted
The poppy stands there shivering in the wind.
But with its red glow of courage
For the grieving wives and children
Who have lost their dads, brothers and uncles
The poppy brings hope.

Nicola Turnbull (11)
Dunino Primary School

FRIENDSHIP

A friend is wonderful
A friend is helpful
A friend is fun
A friend is the one.
A friend you can trust
A friendship will never bust
A friend likes to share
A friend will always be there.

A friend is forever.

Ailsa Turnbull (9)
Dunino Primary School

PARROTS DO ANYTHING

Parrots do anything
Eat anything
Sleep anywhere
Colourful creatures they are
Sharp claws
Sharp beaks
Say anything they hear
They are mimics
They will do
Anything!

Jamie Cruickshank (9)
East Wemyss Primary School

ELEPHANTS

Elephants squirt water furiously.
They are very big and very heavy.
Elephants live in very hot places
And some big rainforests.
Elephants like to sleep and sleep.
You never know what comes next.
All he does is watch TV text.
Elephants try to catch piranhas
But keep getting killed.
Elephants jump in the sand
And always get tanned.

Gordon Ferguson (8)
East Wemyss Primary School

CHEETAHS

Cheetahs run fast,
Cheetahs are daft,
Cheetahs have spots,
Cheetahs have dots,
Look like a tiger,
And almost like fire.

Lewis Ferguson (9)
East Wemyss Primary School

TIGER

As a tiger hunts for meat,
He roars upon his big flat feet.
He always knows if someone's there,
Big or small, long or tall.
Any size he still has eyes
To hunt upon his big flat feet.
Tigers swim in any pond,
In any river - it makes me quiver.
Just before the day ends,
He'll snore in his sleep.

Jessica Henderson (8)
East Wemyss Primary School

PARROTS

Parrots are colourful
They fly anywhere at all
Some parrots have colours
Like red, yellow, blue, white and also green
They have sharp claws.

Tracy Nicol (9)
East Wemyss Primary School

THE LION

A lion roars
It will roar at you
Roar at me
Roar at anyone.

Jordan Peebles (9)
East Wemyss Primary School

KOMODO DRAGON RIPS HIS MEAT

Komodo dragon rips his meat
Sitting down in his seat.
Ripping up his little rabbit,
I wonder how he got to grab it.

Chewing, munching up his meal,
Seeing if anyone dare to steal.
Watching carefully across the land,
Seeing if anyone is in the sand.

Almost finished, nearly done,
He'll probably catch another one.
He is done, sleepy head,
He is getting into bed.

Daniel Sloss (9)
East Wemyss Primary School

PIRANHAS

Piranhas can bite like a tiger
Swim like a fish
They can eat you in twenty seconds flat
Leaving nothing but bones.
So if you see a piranha pool
Never put a finger in
Or -
No finger for you!

Craig Varney (9)
East Wemyss Primary School

LEOPARD'S PREY

Leaping through the forest
Eating all its prey
Picking every piece of it
Or even leaving it lying
Roaring at who comes near him
Dashing all away
Simply even chasing far away.

Pouncing all over the place
Running very fast
Everywhere he goes he jumps
Yes, oh yes, oh yes.

Stephen Watson (9)
East Wemyss Primary School

TIGERS SLEEP ANYWHERE

Tigers sleep
Anywhere
Any house
Anywhere
Even a warm cage will do
Tigers sleep
Anywhere.

Rhiannon Williams (9)
East Wemyss Primary School

DOLPHINS

A dolphin swims anywhere,
Round and round, up and down,
Calling lovely music all around the sea.
But when in danger from some sharks,
It is time to accelerate back
Across the sea.
A dolphin swims anywhere.

Ross Wilson (9)
East Wemyss Primary School

MY PETS

I have two cats and one dog.
The cats like to chase each other's tails.
Our dog likes to chase the cat's tail too.
One cat is Lucky and the other is Tahitti.
Our dog is Holly
And they all eat each other's food.

Kerry Johnstone (8)
Guardbridge Primary School

MY ANIMALS

My pet is called Jet,
She is my favourite pet.
I have other pets
But Jet is the best.
I take her for walks,
We both enjoy it,
It is fun.
My favourite animals are dogs,
My dog is funny when she is excited.

Natasha McDonald (9)
Guardbridge Primary School

—

MRS KENT

Mrs Kent is my teacher
And she is a wonderful feature.
She sits at her desk
And marks our maths test.

Mrs Kent loves cats
And wears funny hats.
She likes dogs
And wears nice clogs.

She has some luck
And buys things from tuck.
We are sometimes a pest
But she's the very best.

Leanne Chalmers (9)
Guardbridge Primary School

WHAT A WONDERFUL WORLD

The sun is shining in the sky
And little birds flying high.
No clouds in the sky,
What a wonderful world.

Children playing in the park
And children watching Noah's Ark.
Dogs going *bark, bark, bark,*
What a wonderful world.

The sun setting in the sky
And children saying goodbye.
It's getting dark now,
The day is over, the night is nigh.
What a wonderful world.

Sarah McClements (9)
Guardbridge Primary School

MY NEW BIKE

My new bike has ten gears,
Maybe five, but hey! Who cares!
I want to ride it oh so much
And Mummy says 'OK.'
I ride all around the street,
I race a train,
I race a car.
My watch has struck two o'clock!
Time for lunch.
I played all day,
It got very dark.
It is nine o'clock.
I went to bed,
That very night
I said 'Goodnight.'

Andrew Kiernan (8)
Guardbridge Primary School

THE WORLD

The world is such a wonderful place
Full of charm, full of grace.
But is the world such a dream?
For children - endless amounts of cream.
Or for adults - money! *Hooray!*
And to sit and pass the day.
Dream? It isn't. It's full of war.
Greediness. There's the rich, there's the poor.
So is the world such a good place?
No! It's not full of charm and grace!
The world is an unfair place.

Jenny Smith (11)
Milnathort Primary School

MY GRANDAD'S GARDEN

My grandad's garden is the best,
it's nothing like all the rest.
With a beautiful bird bath for birds to bathe
and a wishing well for the rain water to save.

With rows of beautiful roses,
with different colours and scents,
when it gets windy they always bend,
that's why he ties them up to a fence.
My grandad's garden is the best.

With all his flower pots, tools and mower,
Granny says he'll probably get some more,
with them stored neatly in his shed,
Granny says he should sleep in there instead of his bed!

In the winter nothing much happens in Grandad's garden,
he says to Granny it is too cold thank heavens,
in the spring he plants the bulbs and the seeds,
in the summer he pulls out all the weeds,
he never lazes or takes a rest,
that's why Grandad's garden is the best.

With all his pruning and cutting the grass,
when planting and weeding he's at his best,
that's why his garden's better than the rest.

After a long day in the garden he's sore and tired,
it's time to sit by the flickering log fire,
when he settles to watch the telly,
he rests his big hands on his fat belly.

As the dusk turns into night,
he thinks of his garden - what a great sight.
He knows I think his garden is best,
because my grandad is better than the rest.

Amy Fowler (10)
Milnathort Primary School

HANSEL AND GRETEL

Hansel and Gretel are great,
They got into a terrible state,
They got chucked out at night
and got a big fright.
Poor Hansel and Gretel.

'Mmm' look at that candy house,
The boy Hansel one day did say,
But look at that house it's the
home of a mouse,
'Why don't we explore it today?'

But that house was the home of a witch,
On her head had a very big stick,
She took them aside and said,
'Hey, come inside!'

Ha, ha, big mistake, anyway.

Hansel and Gretel are great,
They got into a terrible state,
The witch wanted to eat them day by day
But they packed their bags and ran away.
And if you asked them if they wanted to stay,
All you'll hear from them is 'No way.'

Rhona Grant (11)
Milnathort Primary School

WEATHER

The rain falls on the window
Drip, drop.
It shimmers and shines
Plip, plop.
It reflects the light
This cold winter's night
Sending shadows ablaze.

The wind whips at the window,
Roar, bang.
It howls and destroys
Roar, plang.
It steals all the light
This cold winter's night
Sending shadows into a daze.

All this is happening right overhead
While I am warm and snug in my bed
Watching the rain splash
Hearing the wind whine
Drifting to sleep
With a shiver down my spine.

Charlotte Graham (12)
Milnathort Primary School

SCHOOL

School is a happy place,
Kids running with smiles on their face,
All the teachers join in the race,
School is a happy place.

The boys are playing football on the grass,
Oh! What a wonderful pass!
They stopped the game and made their way back to class,
'The bell's about to ring!' said a wee lass.

The bell rang and in they go,
Standing on the teachers' toe,
Then she shouts 'Watch how you go!'
'You have just flattened my big toe!'

Suzanne Blackadder (11)
Milnathort Primary School

Up, Up And Away

There was a wee man in a plane,
That wanted to fly to Spain,
He tried on the first,
But failed of thirst
And then it started to rain.

He tried the next day,
But went the wrong way
And then he said 'Go away.'

For he tried the next day
And said he wanted to stay,
Yes stay, yes stay, yes stay
And said he wanted to stay,
Yes stay, yes stay.

Caitlin Wilkinson (9)
Milnes Primary School

WORLDLY FEAR

The sun is dimming, dying
Children are sobbing, crying.
Men and women drop a single tear
The world is full of deadly fear.

The stars above are failing to shine
A terrified feeling, like never before
Has entered in this heart of mine.

The moon has dropped its beautiful glow,
The well nearby has stopped its flow
All the dogs are forgetting to bark
And so, World War Three has made its mark.

Natasha Cervantes (10)
Portmoak Primary School

NIGHT TO DAY

It's getting dark, the night has come
Hello moon, goodbye sun.
The sky is black with silver stars
On the road there are no cars.
   Night to day, Night to day

In pitch black, forest trees stand tall
As time goes by rain starts to fall
From stony caves fly big, black bats
On the ground, prowl alley cats.
   Night to day, Night to day

Night time is over, the sun is here
Daylight has come, morning is near.
Trees stand proudly, branches long
Colourful birds sing their song.
   Night to day, Night to day

Rachel Robertson (10)
Portmoak Primary School

OUR WORLD

Our world is such a terrible place,
With wars and battles,
The human race is disappearing fast,
There's no place to run, nowhere to hide.

Flee with your children,
Run like the wind,
All you people who have sinned,
Beware the darkness is coming in.

Our pollution is affecting the atmosphere,
We will melt with a ray of the sun,
So all beware the darkness of evil,
Shall command our world forever.

But we have hope ahead of us,
One ray of light brightens the darkness,
If we look after our world we will survive,
But if we don't evil will command.

Recycle your rubbish,
Don't throw it in the bin,
Give old clothes to charity
And remember, never sin,
For the darkness will catch you.

Look at our world, isn't it better?
We have won the war
And saved our world.

Lauren Gentry (10)
Portmoak Primary School

NIGHT-TIME

When night-time comes and darkness falls
Another world appears.
The moon is lit with the stars above
A chill to everyone's fears.

The earth is silent, the breeze is low
And nothing is to be heard.
Until the sun comes up again
And wakes the early bird.

Timothy Pryde (10)
Portmoak Primary School

DARKNESS

When the dark takes over the land
And everything goes black
Darkness reigns
Its sinister appearance
Strikes fear in people's hearts
But the strange thing about it
It doesn't scare me.

I feel relaxed in the dark
I can't see the danger
Darkness is mistaken,
Darkness is not a thing to be scared of
Darkness rules!

David Mackenzie (10)
Portmoak Primary School

THE MUTANT WASHING MACHINE

The mutant washing machine lived under the stairs,
With bright red eyes it slowly glares.
I don't like this stupid thing,
At twelve o'clock noon, it always goes 'ding'.

The mutant washing machine lived under the stairs,
And it has lots of coloured flares.
It is always singing a strange, silly song,
At twelve o'clock midnight, it always goes 'dong'.

The mutant washing machine lived under the stairs,
Where it still strangely stares.
It never ate any food,
Surely, now it has gone for good!

Robert Cail (10)
Portmoak Primary School

I'M GLAD I'M NOT THAT

I'm glad I'm not that bumble bee
Buzzing around, in and out that tree
Not even allowed to write a letter
To make my honey a little better.

I'm glad I'm not that army of ants
Going up the leg of people's pants!
Imagine working all day
Not even allowed to go out to play.

I'm glad I'm not that kangaroo
Hopping and jumping in that zoo
Or crowded in that little space
Where he can't take a big pace.

I'm glad I'm what I am
And my name isn't Tom
I'm just a boy
That's all I am.

Shaun Masson (10)
Portmoak Primary School

MY DOG

I lie in my bed just staring at her,
An adorable sight.
I lie in my bed morning and night.
Looking at my dog.

She loves lots of attention.
She likes to play with squeaky toys.
She loves to play and run around.
She likes to play with other dogs especially boys.

I love to play with my dog.
I love to feed my dog.
I love to hug my dog.
But most of all I like to love my dog.

Johny Hain (10)
Portmoak Primary School

MY PUZZLE DOG

Soft, cuddly, really cute
Black, brown and gold
I wonder if you've guessed
My dog's name and breed
I'll give you a clue, it starts with 'I',
What, no not eye, but 'I;,
What, no not me 'I . . .N . . .D . . .Y'
Indy the German Shepherd (Alsatian).

Rob Drysdale (10)
Portmoak Primary School

THE DOG

I love to do this

I am a golden labrador
My name is Nala
I jump and run all day long but mainly I fade away.

I love to do this

I'll play with you if you play with me
If you don't, I'll stay away.

I love to do this

Sometimes I am good
Sometimes I am bad
But I try really hard not to be bad.

I love to do this

Bounce, chase balls and sticks
But when you look at me I run away.

I love to do this

Pounce and bark
Because it keeps me awake all day.

I love to do this.

I like humans
But especially children
Because they play with me.

Elizabeth Todd (9)
Portmoak Primary School

STORMY

If you want a dog
Forget about your mog.
Just call in your nearest pound
And get yourself a hound.

We are going, we are going
To see what we can get
A labrador or a cocker spaniel
We could name it Daniel.

They are all so cute and loving
They're saying please pick me
But wait and see
We will go get the key
To open up the door.

We have chosen
To name her Stormy
My little cocker spaniel
We could have named her Daniel
But that's not good for a girl.

Lissie Kennedy (10)
Portmoak Primary School

THE WEATHER MONSTERS

Morning sunshine is so clear,
That's when the weather monsters appear.

Two suns as eyes,
A cloud as a hair,
A raindrop for a head,
A rainbow mouth,
A twister body,
A sunset cheek of red.

Lightning eyebrows flash across his face,
His voice is thunder booming in space.

When he's frustrated he is mean.
A splitting headache weather machine.
When he is satisfied, he is kind.
A calm and gentle force of mind.

He loves to act in secret,
With giant lightning bolts,
He eats crusts of stars,
That make him play with volts.

Flying through the open space,
Shooting stars, an utter chase.
Whizzing around the battered earth,
The weather monster rushes for all he's worth.

Back down through the atmosphere,
His favourite game,
Is stirring up wind into a hurricane.

But the sun is setting,
He has to go to rewrite the weather
With a different pen.
To have his fun again.

James Foreman (10)
Portmoak Primary School

SALLY

Sally is a dog who is very kind
She needs a lot of attention, bear in mind.
Don't be shocked if she does the toilet in the house
It might be she's seen a mouse.

Sally walks three times a day
She needs feeding morning, noon and night.
Sally loves five treats a day
She needs to be cared for all the time.

She uses a basket to sleep on at night
Remember she will never bite.
When she's in the shower
She thinks she's got a lot of power.

Sally doesn't like water
She only likes milk.
Sally loves going for walks
Especially in the wood.

You know how she loves walks
She doesn't like it when her owner talks
One day she ate a beef bone
In the hall we heard a groan.

Sally is a girl
She is nine years old
Her favourite food is chicken bones
She is a golden retriever.

Fiona Stratton (9)
Portmoak Primary School

MY DOG BOUNCER

Bouncer is brown with a bit of black
You can cuddle him but not go for a hack.

When he's wet he gets quite smelly
But when it comes to pudding on our plate
He can smell the jelly.

He's nice to cuddle at night
But comes under the blanket
When he gets a fright.

When you need someone to talk to
He's always there for you.

When he has a shower
He takes longer than an hour.

He is shaggy not raggy.

He is a gentle soul
But can knock down a pole
With a strike of his paw.

He likes to go for a walk
But cannot talk.

He likes to play with babies
And doesn't have rabies.

He is full of trust, not hate
And believe me his colour's like rust.

He is always listening!

Woof, Woof.

Amber Ainsworth (9)
Portmoak Primary School

THE BUTTERFLY

One day up in the trees
I saw a butterfly smiling at me.
I climbed up the tree
Then I fell down
I realised it was flying around me
Then it was shining on me.
It said 'I will grant you three wishes.'
So I said 'I wish I didn't have to do any work again.'
So I went in and mum told me to do my homework
Then I quickly rushed outside and I found my brother
I said 'You played a trick on me,' but he just laughed.

Joshua Haslam (9)
Portmoak Primary School

THE SUN

The sun is bright and red
Every morning when I get out of bed.
Sometimes it's raining and sunny
A rainbow comes, that's funny.
A sunset is beautiful
Sunrise is too.
And so is the sun
When the sky's pale blue.

Paul Soutar (8)
St Agatha's Primary School, Leven

THE SUN

The sun is bright, it is so light.
The sun is red, it gets me out of bed.
I like the sun in the summer
When I go out for picnics.
The sun is really happy
It makes me happy too.
In the evening it's like it's blood in the sky
The sun is big and yellow.
It reminds me of a desert
When you see an oasis, you feel so good.
It covers up the moon.
When lying in bed, it shines in my window
You can sunbathe on the beach
But you might get sunburnt.

Craig Ratcliffe (8)
St Agatha's Primary School, Leven

THE RED SUN

I love the sun it makes me hot when I'm in my bed.
In the evening the sun looks like blood in the sky
When it is setting.
I like the sun in the summer
When I am in the pool.
I love the sun
It makes me very happy.

Jennifer Dickson (8)
St Agatha's Primary School, Leven

THE SUN

I love the sun because it makes me happy.
I love the sun when it shines down on Earth.
I love the sun because it is beautiful.
The sun is a big ball of fire.
I love the sun when I am at the pool.
I hate it when I am in school when it is hot.

Mickeala Lindsay (8)
St Agatha's Primary School, Leven

THE SUN

The sun is red
And gets me out of my bed.
It makes me warm and cosy
It is yellow and round and bright.
I love the sun
It makes me happy.

Carla Boyce (8)
St Agatha's Primary School, Leven

THE SUN

The sun makes me happy
It's so yellow and warm.
It reminds me of the beach when I'm on holiday
You can have a barbecue if the sun is bright.
I love the sun.

The sun is so big and round
It's the biggest star in the universe.
It's the brightest light on Earth
The sun brings the birds out to sing.
I love the sun.

The sun reminds me of a desert
Soaking up pools, making you unhappy.
The sun is scorching hot in Africa
In the evening it's like the sun is dying.
I love the sun.

Craig Bullions (8)
St Agatha's Primary School, Leven

THE SUN

The sun makes me get out of my bed.
The sun makes me happy
And the sun is like a big ball of fire.
It shines on the earth
And I think the sun is beautiful.

Michael Lee (8)
St Agatha's Primary School, Leven

THE SUN

The sun is hot and warm
The sun is yellow and red
The sun is big and round
The sun is like a lemon
The sun makes me and the birds happy.

The sun is a big star
The sun can dry up water
The sun is far, far away
The birds love the sun,
So do I!
The sun is brighter than lights
And fire put together.
I love the sun
More than it loves me.

Declan Stevens (8)
St Agatha's Primary School, Leven

DEEP IN SPACE

All the twinkling stars
glowing and shining
in the gasses that burn inside them.

The golden planets orbiting the sun
as the sunlight shines upon them.

Hot, hot sunlight, 600°C

Black holes dark and low
deep, deep in space.

Rockets launching from earth
figuring out fascinating facts
about . . .
Space!

Maria Connelly (9)
St Columba's Primary School, Cupar

SNOW

Snow is a winter wonderland,
Snow is a glistening carpet over the world,
Snow is droplets on the twinkling trees,
Snow cracks my mum's plant pots,
Snow lets the bears know when to hibernate,
Snow makes your nose feel tingly,
Snow floats down like soft, tickly feathers.

Claudia Fusaro (9)
St Columba's Primary School, Cupar

MOON

M an in the Moon

O rbiting the Earth

O pening the night

N ice and bright!

Vanessa Murray (9)
St Columba's Primary School, Cupar

AUTUMN

The leaves of autumn
Crunchy, crispy,
All different colours.

The flame of bonfire night
Light and flickering.

The squirrels crunching on the leaves
While they look for acorns to eat.

The pumpkins of Hallowe'en
Very scary they may seem!

Douglas Williams (9)
St Columba's Primary School, Cupar

URANUS

U nusual is this blue gas giant
R esting near the edge of the solar system
A different axis from the other planets
N ever warm, away from the sun
U p in the universe, on its own, lonely
S ilent lies Uranus.

Stephen MacColl (9)
St Columba's Primary School, Cupar

NIGHT

Night is crystal, cool air
Night is a peaceful time
Night is a sleepy time
Night is a dream world
Night is a rustling hedgehog
Night is my snoring dad
Night is my favourite time.

Mark Brown (9)
St Columba's Primary School, Cupar

SNOW

Snow falls from the sky
Squidgy, soft
Comes at Christmas
Very white, very cold.
Red fingers
Red hands
Makes me shiver
As if I'm nervous.

Tarik Kssiaa (9)
St Columba's Primary School, Cupar

SPACE

S olar system, full of planets

P robes, searching into space

A steroids roaming, crashing everywhere

C omets, whizzing like dirty snowballs

E arth is lucky to have space.

Kim Blyth (9)
St Columba's Primary School, Cupar

SPACE

All the sparkly stars twinkle and glow
in a sheet of black mist.
All the golden planets sparkling and crisp
satellites whiz by.
Rocket launching from the earth,
the sun crisping and burning
like a fiery lion's mane.

Amy McKenzie (9)
St Columba's Primary School, Cupar

MY WEEKLY POEM

On Monday it was a frosty day
So I stayed inside all day.

On Tuesday I was watching TV
Eating chocolate and drinking tea.

On Wednesday I went out to play
And I fell in a heap of crunchy leaves.

On Thursday it was a better day
So I played out with my friends for the day.

On Friday it was bonfire night
And the fireworks burst out in flames.

On Saturday night the sky was grey
And squirrels were climbing up the trees.

On Sunday Dad came home and said
'Pick up all those colourful leaves.'

Amanda Hayes (9)
St Columba's Primary School, Cupar

MY AUTUMN POEM

Autumn sky is blue and white
I think it's rather a pretty sight.
A nice cool breeze on an autumn day
Brings the children out to play.
Ripe, red apples sitting in the tree
Oh go on Mum can I have one please?
Harvest time is nearly here
Combine harvester is coming near.
I hope that I have made it clear
That autumn is the best time of the year.

Ella Mackinnon (9)
St Columba's Primary School, Cupar

NIGHT

Night is the wolf howling in the moon's light
Night is water sparkling and clear,
Night is crystal stars in the dark sky
Night is a quiet time,
People gazing up above
Night is the hedgehog rustling in the bushes
Bats screeching in the trees
Night is the cold wind touching your face.

Callum McLaughlin (9)
St Columba's Primary School, Cupar

CHIMP CHEWS

Cute, dark eyes,
Hairy fingers like us
Holding on
Eating hungrily.

Karis Walker (9)
St Columba's Primary School, Cupar

THE CHEETAH

Hungrily like Homer Simpson
Watchfully like a guarding soldier
Proudly like a famous scientist
The cheetah surveys.

Andrew Stewart (9)
St Columba's Primary School, Cupar

SPACE

S   pace is the final frontier
P   lanets sit comfortably
A   dventure lies beyond our universe
C   omets crashing everywhere
E   verything waiting for us to find.

Fiona McHardy (9)
St Columba's Primary School, Cupar

RED IS . . .

Red is the autumn leaves
Falling to the ground.

Red is the ripened apple
Ready for me to eat.

Red is the lovely roses
That I plant in my garden.

Red is the warm sunset
So colourful and peaceful.

Red is the rose hips
Falling to the ground.

Red is the juicy strawberries
Ready to be picked.

Amy Caldwell (9)
St Columba's Primary School, Cupar

WHEN WILL SNOW COME?

When will snow come drifting down silently?
When will snow come pitter, pattering down?
When will snow come calm and clear?
When oh when will snow come?
When will snow come glittering and shining?
When will snow come with its frostbiting coldness?
When will snow come swirling down?
When oh when will snow come?
Snow has come at last, yippee!
On Christmas Day, it's a gift for me!

Anna Haldane (9)
St Columba's Primary School, Cupar

MY CAT FLAN

I tickle Flan's tum
She purrs just like an engine
Then runs away - Swoosh!

Sam McGlashan (9)
St Columba's Primary School, Cupar

VICTORIAN WRITING

Wearing a cloud-white ink bib
Covering crisp, clean pinny
Inkwell very black and dirty
A never-ending tunnel
Handwriting
Dip for tiniest bit of ink
On metal nib
Swirly, twirly writing
Victorian writing is extremely hard to do!

Alexandra Addison-Scott (9)
St Katharines School, St Andrews

BLACK AND WHITE CAT

Black and white,
Soft and fluffy,
Warm and cuddly,
Tame and loveable,
She smells of pure mist,
Fragile cat, fast asleep.

Fiona Houston (8)
St Katharines School, St Andrews

MY GRANDMA'S CAT

My grandma's cat is a marmalade cat
His real name is too complicated to say.
So we call him Puss Puss
Blue eyes, soft peaceful cat.
He sits on beds and lets you stroke him.
He purrs very softly when he is peaceful.
He purrs like a contented bee that has got honey.
In the winter he will sit by the stove
In his wooden box
And purr and purr.

Lucinda Alderson (8)
St Katharines School, St Andrews

THE FUTURE

It goes on forever
Two thousand makes me think of flying cars
Robots ruling the world
And electric pets.
It makes me feel warm and happy
It makes me feel that in any weather
I can go out and play.

Kirsty Paterson (8)
St Katharines School, St Andrews

THE CROW AND HER NEW CHILD

The new mother sits,
on her waiting child.
Terrified at the moment,
when it will arrive.
Suddenly a push tells
her to get out of the way,
Because the arrival is coming
of the new baby.

Then the infant gives a push
and the shell breaks apart.
He sees a bright light
and his mother gives him a 'Swark!'
Then he gives her a rather weak
tiny little 'squeak!'

Now the crow is living happily
with her little family.
The End

Frances Waterbury (8)
St Katharines School, St Andrews

THE FUTURE

The future makes me feel
dark
black
different
mechanical.
It will be so strange
It is just like things have to be rearranged
And changed
There will be
Robots, flying cars
Yellow chocolate bars.
It will make you feel like you're in Mars
That's what the future is to me.

Sofia Berkhout (8)
St Katharines School, St Andrews

FROG FUTURE

In the past I was an egg with lots of others.
I hatched in the year 1991.
I turned into a tadpole.
Months later I had feet and hands.
In the future I will be a frog policeman
Patrol Toadpole Town
The future is all mine.

Katie Dobell (8)
St Katharines School, St Andrews

THE WORLD IS GOING

The world is going
but no-one is knowing
aliens are coming to kill and to slaughter
the future is cruel as aliens drink down their glorter.

They fire their lasers
killing us one by one
then crash down to earth
weighing a ton.

Was it the pollution or nuclear power?

We do not understand
we ourselves already were dying slower and slower.

Everyone is dead
its a total dearth
except for a kitten
who slipped in a hole under the earth.

I got out the next day
into the morning sun
with rabbits and badgers
to me the world had just begun.

Rory Hunter (11)
St Katharines School, St Andrews

MY FUTURE JOB

My future job may be
An astronaut out to see
More planets in another galaxy
Or even be an architect of an artificial sea.

My future job may be designing high-tech clothes
Or maybe the creator of a paper-thin laptop computer
Or even a time machine.

My future job may be a mother of the 20th century
Like a mother many branches back down the family tree.

Heloise Thomson (10)
St Katharines School, St Andrews

THE LAST SCHOOL OPEN

The last school open,
The last day today.
No school,
No work, no exams in May.

Computers for you,
No books to read.
No pencils to write with,
No need for help.

A digital world,
Ruled over our minds,
No school, just computers for you.

Alexandra Bethune (11)
St Katharines School, St Andrews

THE LONELY MAN

In the future
there will be a man
standing on a hill top
freezing to death,
no food, no home
standing on the hill top
all alone.

He felt lonely
no one to go to
he was a lonely man
left on Earth
only man on Earth
the only person on Earth.

The lonely man
the lonely man of Earth
a shooting bomb
flying across the foggy sky
killing everyone
except the lonely man.

Laura Angus (10)
St Katharines School, St Andrews

THE FUTURE

Spaceships, laser guns.
Holidays to the sun.
Journeys to Jupiter
Everybody's having fun.

Big guns, laser guns.
Canons everywhere.
Space mutants in their ships
Flying everywhere.

Spaceships in the air
Everybody, everywhere.
Having fun on the sun
And Jupiter and Mars.

Big guns, laser guns.
Friends in outer space.
Pain and suffering - in disgrace.
Lost in outer space.

Spaceships, laser guns.
Happiness everywhere.
Perfect people with no hair.
Loving - everywhere.

Andrew Johnston (11)
St Katharines School, St Andrews

FROZEN

Gazing out the window watching seconds tick by,
What would the earth be in ten years time?
My children could be computerised robots, or worse,
When I die they might freeze me,
Use me as a scientific experiment then,
In a thousand years time defrost me,
I would wander round like a zombie.
Unaware that robots now ruled the world,
A man's no longer anywhere in the universe,
The king of the planet would catch me, put me in a cage,
I would be an exhibition
Relying on metal bars for food, acid as drink,
But I cannot live my life in fear.

Sarah Hartland-Mahon (12)
St Katharines School, St Andrews

FUTURE 3000

Concrete flats
are way up there,
Smoke and car fumes
in the air.
Power stations, fact'ries
roam the land,
No more fields, grass or sand.

Robot teachers
robot friends,
Internet shopping
E-mail sends.
No more homework
schools are gone,
English, maths
now a CD Rom.

Knarled and crooked
that is me,
Grey hair, hearing aid
and false teeth.
A metal walking stick
in my hand,
Sorry for the world
a digital land.

Margaret Houston (11)
St Katharines School, St Andrews

WWW.Futurelifeafterdeath.Com

My life, rusted
Will soon be forgotten
When my spaceship is blasted
To the moon.

The world, disappearing
As I sit there dying
With no contact for help
On the moon.

When I am dead
I will hover round for decades
Until like a butterfly on a summer's day rainbow
I will become.

Back from the moon
I will flutter
To a new world.

No moon in sight
Just graphic, multimedia processors
I will type:
www.futurelifeafterdeath.com was here!

Louise Easton (11)
St Katharines School, St Andrews

WHY ARE ALIENS CALLED ALIENS?

Why are aliens called aliens?

Maybe because of their flying saucers
Big and round
Flashing lights
Imagine if you went up there
Stars sparkling in your eyes.

Why are aliens called aliens?

I know,
Their round mysterious eyes
That you can look straight through
Galaxies flowing in and out of their pupils.

But why are aliens called aliens?

Helena Berkhout (11)
St Katharines School, St Andrews

SPACE

Like a swimming pool of air,
Vacation to space,
A one day return fare.
See the Martians playing tentacle ball,
Endless competition as the ball cannot fall.

Pop into Pluto for lunch;
The gravity helps you munch.
Time to go home,
Take the planet express,
Two more stars before planet Earth.

Andrew Bradley (11)
St Katharines School, St Andrews

GATEWAY TO THE FUTURE

I can see the future.
My crystal ball like a gateway
I elevate my hands
Place them on the mystic ball
At first hazy.
Then a crystalline picture of the days to come.
Things seem different.
Deserted landscapes
Nothing there
Nothing wanted
Nothing at all.

Alyson McKechnie (11)
St Katharines School, St Andrews

A GIFT NOT A CURSE

In my dreams, I see
What could happen to you or me.
If they believed me,
I could save a bank, a house.
You would be able to become healthy,
You won't die,
I could make a cure for horrible diseases.

But nobody believes me.
I'm not clever, just a threat,
But seeing the future
Is a gift, not a curse.

Sarah Stewart (11)
St Katharines School, St Andrews

STILL TIME

What would happen if life forgot about the future,
threw away the watches, let time stand still?
Never to think 'What do I have to do next?'
Just lie,
under the sunny sky.
On a sandy beach
near a clear, blue sea.
That would be the life for me.

Kirsten Donaldson (11)
St Katharines School, St Andrews

THE BLASTED OAK

Morning has risen after beautiful night,
Will it be the same tonight?
The stately oak tree standing strong and tall,
Branches long and wide,
With golden, yellow leaves all around.

Hearing children laughing, playing in the forest,
Drips of rain slowly drops,
As the laughing stops,
Children return to their houses to keep warm and dry,
As the rain continues,
A storm follows on.

Lightning flashes,
Thunder rumbles,
But the silver twinkle of the moon can still be seen,
Even as the rain gets heavier and heavier,
And as it continues through the night,
Getting worse and worse.

Morning strikes,
All is quiet.

The summering sun shines,
But the shrivelled skeleton, smoked in shadow,
When the children come out to play,
Astonishment fills the forest,
By the blasted oak tree.

Andrea Kilgour (12)
St Katharines School, St Andrews

SNOW WOLF

Snowy wolf with a soft, white coat
Howling on the edge of a cliff
Running off to his family of young

Mouth
Slimy mouth
A sly smile

Eyes
Yellow glowing eyes
A piercing glare as if to say
'Don't come near me'

Ears
Fluffy and white
Pointed like spikes

Home
A cold black den
Not big, not small

Wolf's mind
'I am nice and cosy
I want to go to sleep
Sweet dreams.'

Rachel Coleman (9)
St Katharines School, St Andrews

FUTURE FASHION

Future woman

Dresses made of plastic
Coded pockets
Invisible to the naked eye
Press a button
And do the machanana
And the dress will become short

Future man

Man with eye earrings
Spring in their heels
Zip, zap, zam
The sounds of the laser belts fighting
Their clothes will be electric
Blue and sharp.

Merle Henderson (9)
St Katharines School, St Andrews

THE TIME MACHINE

There it is, standing there
All alone
I cannot bear it
All alone
So I get in
There is no one there
Just me
It shines so bright
I cannot wait!
I have to go!
So off I go
Just me!

Its stone-cold levers
Crash, bang! Off I go!
Just me
Then suddenly
Right out of the ozone layer I go!
I miss some planets
I am so excited
Just me
All alone

Just me
Hear my mum calling me
There it ended, or was it a
                    dream?

Lorenna Hunter (9)
St Katharines School, St Andrews

THE FUTURE

I arrive at the fair
The rocket sits there
It gleams in the sun
It looks such fun
I get in the rocket
It zooms up in the air
Two seconds gone
I am in space
I go in and out of the twinkling stars
Looking at
Burning Mars
Calm Venus
Red-hot Jupiter
The gleaming moon.

2, 3, 4 headed creatures
5, 6, 7 armed creatures
8, 9, 10-legged creatures

I climb into my rocket
It bursts into the air
Whizz round Mars, almost there
Zoom through Mercury, even closer
I land on Earth
I see lots of ugly creatures
All walking, talking and looking
Only I face, two legs and two arms.

I climb into the rocket
It zooms into the air
The end of another adventurous day.

Poppy Diana Open (10)
St Katharines School, St Andrews

CUB

Lovely fur
Want one as a pet
Beautiful, gentle brown eyes
The way he moves is lovely to see
Little wolf curls up with me
Like a tiny baby

Ready to eat his meat
Your daddy's dripping jaws
Knowing he won't hurt me
Staring at you from a far distance
Crying when lonely
Crying wolf tears

Pricked-up ears
Listening for footsteps
Very silent
Hiding in a bush
He wants someone to love him
Crying wolf tears
He's feeling that I'm the right
          person to care for him
And, I *will* protect him.

Helen Coleman (8)
St Katharines School, St Andrews

THE PHOTO

What is going to happen?
A baby growing into a child.
An author writes in the future
A new book.
For the people reading the book
It will be the present
My baby sister didn't know
At Christmas
What was happening
At all
But next year . . .

This year she was
Climbing up all the presents
Piled on the couch
Mummy took a photo
It will be old
When she is one
It will be old just now
When it is being printed
It will be the past
But now it is the present.

Joanna Brown (9)
St Katharines School, St Andrews

SHUTTLE TO PLUTO

A shuttle is coming
To take me to Pluto
Everyone is running
To catch the shuttle
The shuttle to Pluto

The next one will be here
At the station on the moon
It is coming in two light years
We have to catch the shuttle
The shuttle to Pluto

At last we reach it
We are strapped in our seats
At last the engines are lit
We are on the shuttle
The shuttle to Pluto

I can't wait to get there
To see a nogtipus
Or a giant nilumipere
I can't wait to get off the shuttle
The shuttle to Pluto

At last it reaches the station
I can see Pluto at last
Before I've used my imagination
We jump off the shuttle
The shuttle to Pluto

There are animals of all kinds
Samyurs, Milopuses, Moditites
There are even Samalinds
We walk away from the shuttle
The shuttle to Pluto.

Rowan Mackenzie-Kennedy
St Katharines School, St Andrews

COOL COLOURS

Red is the colour of roses.
I water them with hoses.

Red are the feathers on my parrot.
His favourite food is carrots.

Yellow is the colour of the sun,
Shining down when we're having fun.

Yellow is the colour of sand.
I like to hold it in my hand.

Yellow is the colour of buzzing bees,
Making honey puts their minds at ease.

Pink is the colour of my room.
I clean it with a broom.

Ferne Dair (10)
St Ninian's Primary School, Cardenden

COLOURS OF THE WORLD

Red is the colour of the sun
The day is over, we've had a lot of fun.

Red is the colour of the fire. It burns.
We all sing round it taking turns.

Red is the colour of the leaves,
When they start to fall out of the trees.

Red is the colour of the Man United strip
'Come on Man United, hey, Ref, that was a trip!'

Red is the colour of a lovely red rose.
As soon as I sniff it, a bee goes up my nose.

Deonne Currie (10)
St Ninian's Primary School, Cardenden

POETRY

Parents usually say -
Quit chewing chewing gum
Stop watching TV
Go to the shops
Get off your bum.

Go to the shops
Move your toys
Hurry, get a move on
Don't fight with boys.

It's not fair,
It's always me
It's boring,
It wasn't just me.

> Don't make me go to the shops.
> You go instead.
> Don't tell me off
> Don't tell me to go to bed.

> Do give me money
> Do give me toys
> Do make my breakfast
> Some toast and honey.

Kerrie Johnstone (9)
St Ninian's Primary School, Cardenden

DO THIS, DO THAT, DO EVERYTHING

'Must do this,' my mum says.
'Must do that,' my dad says.
It's always me.

'Stop at once,' says my dad.
'Go to the shops,' says my mum.
It's always me.

Here are rules for adults -
Don't worry all day
Don't come in my room
Don't do this. Don't do that.

Do the dishes
Do the shopping all the time.
Do this. Do that.

Roxanne Kerr (10)
St Ninian's Primary School, Cardenden

COLOURS EVERYWHERE

Green are the leaves on a tree.
The leaves fall in the autumn, you can see.

Green are the stripes of my favourite team.
Their football skills are smooth like cream.

Yellow is the colour of a lemon.
In the market they always sell them.

Yellow are the stripes of a bee.
They might sting you and me.

Brown is a big, high wall.
To see over it, you need to be tall.

I have got big, brown shoes.
I wear them to Edinburgh Zoo.

Bryan Duncan (10)
St Ninian's Primary School, Cardenden

WHAT BOSSY PARENTS SAY

My bossy parents say

'Do your hair'
'Stop at once'
'Go for the milk'
'Quit the football'
'Quickly make your bed.'

'Get a move on'
'Move the computer'
'Wait your turn'
'Get the cat in'
'Answer the question'
'Get out of the classroom'
'Don't swear'
'Change your shoes,' and
'What is that?'

I hate being bossed around all the time
It was not me
It's not fair
I always have to do this
It's always me
I tell you, it's always me.

Peter Mellon (10)
St Ninian's Primary School, Cardenden

SCOTLAND

S uch a beautiful landscape
C aledonia we were called
O ver the country, rain pours
T allest mountain in Britain is here
L ots of land, empty and unclaimed
A city of greatness is Edinburgh
N obody will defeat us
D ay, night or ever.

Martin Davidson (11)
St Paul's Primary School, Glenrothes

LOVE

L ove is someone you like
O r someone that's nice to you
V alentines are full of love and laughter
E verybody loves their mum and dad, well,
    I do!

Jade Hamill (11)
St Paul's Primary School, Glenrothes

MY BEST FRIEND

I know a boy, he's my friend
On him I can depend
He's always there to support me
Whatever my trouble may be
He is my *best* friend.

Scott Bell (11)
St Paul's Primary School, Glenrothes

SPIDERS

Creepy-crawly, hairy spiders,
Crawling over the walls,
Make one wrong move, spiders,
And you might just fall,
Creeping over the walls at night
Always giving me a fright,
Why do spiders always bug me?
Well, they are bugs.

Christopher Johnson (11)
St Paul's Primary School, Glenrothes

TREES

T all as buildings,
R eaching for the sky,
E veryone is different,
E ventually they all die,
S waying in every direction.

Natalie O'Donnell (11)
St Paul's Primary School, Glenrothes

CATS

Fur like coal
nose like a snowflake
I watched it
she spotted her prey
and went
very slowly
towards
it
then
she *pounced.*

Hannah Proctor (11)
St Paul's Primary School, Glenrothes

ANIMALS

A nimals are one of the most wonderful things
   in the world,
N ature brings them up and nature puts them down,
I nside, outside, they are everywhere,
M ammals, amphibians, they all come as one,
A ll different types, shapes and sizes,
L oving and caring for each other,
S urviving each day as danger comes.

Vanessa Bronzina (11)
St Paul's Primary School, Glenrothes

WHAT ANIMALS DO

Lions spy
And birds fly.
Lambs leap
Cows all sleep.
Horses neigh,
Whilst sheep eat hay.
Kangaroos jump,
But rhinos thump.
Pigs grunt
And tigers hunt.
Swans glide,
Whilst meerkats hide.
Dogs run fast
But tortoises are last.

That's what animals do.

Laura Kelly (10)
St Paul's Primary School, Glenrothes

DOWN BEHIND THE DUSTBINS

Down behind the dustbins,
I met a bird called Tweety,
I asked him, 'What are you doing?'
He said, 'Sylvester is trying to eat me!'

Sandie McArdle (10)
St Paul's Primary School, Glenrothes

THE WORLD AROUND US

The world around us is big and bold.
It can be very strange you know,
The swamps and jungles are very clammy.
The world has plenty of creatures on it.
Tigers, cats and elephants.
Polar bears at the North Pole.
Avalanches! So cold and powerful.

Trees, so big and beautiful
Skyscrapers that tower over you
I wonder if I'll ever see
The Wonders of the World.
Pyramids, deserts and oases.
The Victoria Falls,
The crashing waters.

Cities, towns and quaint little villages
Big sailing ships and fishing boats.
Buses, cars, trains as well
Telephones and televisions.
Letters and stamps.
They are all part of our world.

The world is dazzling,
With colours gold and silver,
Its beauty cannot be described,
To me or to you.
Water and wind,
Humans and animals
All make up the world.

Look after the world
It is a wonder!

Victoria Beat (9)
Sea View Private School

BIRTHDAYS

Birthdays happen once a year,
You are getting older, my children dear,
Paper rustling as presents are opened,
Children excited and faces glowing,
The noise is loud, I can't be heard,
Where can I go to hide my head?

Out the back the children go,
Jumping and dancing to and fro,
The rain starts pouring down in sheets,
Splashing and splishing with muddy feet,
The children come in soaked to the skin,
Clothes taken off and thrown in the bin.

The barbecue is out and set alight,
Flames roaring, high up into the night,
Wine to drink and food to eat,
It's time for the adults to rest their feet,
The children come down and fall asleep,
They're cuddled up closely like a flock of sheep.

Danielle Robertson (9)
Sea View Private School

WINTER WONDERLAND

Icy white slippery snow,
Cars skidding, children falling,
Mum and Dad howling,
Cold winter nights bring hoar frost,
With crystals out of dewdrops made,
What a sight!

Icy white slippery snow,
Children moulding and sculpturing it like dough,
Grass not needing to be mowed,
Bare trees in the garden,
Holding up what used to be their stardom,
Greenery got a fright!

Icy white slippery snow,
Numb noses and sore toes,
Stepping onto the crunchy snow,
Where the boys sliding and skating go,
The puffy sparrows huddle close,
Lest they freeze.

Icy white slippery snow,
Christmas Eve presents being wrapped,
Children peeking through gaps,
Fairy lights flashing in the morning,
Christmas tree decorations gleaming,
Oh! So bright!

Icy white slippery snow,
Inside my house nice and cosy,
Happy with a hot drink and feeling lazy,
I look outside, gritters coming with their heavy load,
What a way,
To end a day.

Kasim Ahmad (9)
Sea View Private School

OLD TIMES TO NEW TIMES

The year two thousand has arrived just now,
How did we reach it, tell me how?
BC turned to AD,
As Christ was born to make us free,
Will this century go so fast?
Will it have so long to last?

Ten decades passed to make one hundred years,
Then a millennium full of hopes and tears,
This passes so very quickly,
Never standing still for you or me.
Will we learn from mistakes of the past?
Will our careful plans hold fast?

World War One then World War Two,
Not ever a memory for me or you,
Cruel war, then victory,
Peace and time for harmony,
Will war come to plague us again?
Have we learned from tears and pain?

Votes for women, atomic bombs,
Cars, boats, planes and popular songs,
New technology,
Phones, computers,
Filling our lives with exciting futures,
Will these inventions help us cope?
Is this the century full of hope?

The only answer I can give,
Is to care for our world,
The place where we live,
Think ahead and plan for times to come,
Enjoy your life and make time for fun,
Think of your friends and family,
And we will all live together happily.

Rosie Steer (9)
Sea View Private School

A NEW BEGINNING

It's a new beginning
It's a new year
It's time for people to meet everywhere.
There are parties to go to and food to eat.
There's not even time to put up your feet.

It's a new beginning
It's a new year
We spend time with those who are dear
All merry and happy as bright as can be.
There's no one around as lucky as me.

It's a new beginning
It's a new year
Let's think of those living in fear
There's so much trouble, and so much war
There's a lot of suffering, what is it for?

It's a new beginning
It's a new year
We must start to protect the environment here.
Everyone take care not to pollute our land
We must take matters in our very own hand.

It's a new beginning
It's a new year
Let's make a difference, the message is clear.
If we help our neighbours and those further away
The world may be better and peaceful, we pray.

It's a new beginning
It's a new year
And it's time to change, to stop shedding tears.
If children unite and show you the way
The world can be better and peaceful *today!*

Anna Campbell (9)
Sea View Private School

CRICKET

Cricket, once a gentleman's game,
Played first at Lords,
Enjoyed by families,
On sunny summer day,
Watching cricket,
Enjoying a picnic.

Long time ago, England were best,
Australia and India,
Tried their bit,
The West Indies' fast bowlers,
And hard-hitting batsmen,
Beat England.

When the Aussies came to England,
To play a test series,
Their wishes were to win on English soil,
But they lost miserably,
They couldn't take the 'Ashes' home,
England rejoiced joyfully.

One team is having a bad time,
The other is having fun,
Spectators are watching nervously,
To see who wins,
I think cricket's a tense sport,
You never know who will win.

Abdullah Mahmood (9)
Sea View Private School

HALLOWE'EN

Hallowe'en witches ugly and black,
Witches have an old brown sack,
The black smelly cats,
And the grey old rats,
Spells made from frogs,
From the smelly bogs.

A goblin and a demon,
Screaming through the city,
Without any pity,
Aliens from who knows where.
Aliens come to scare,
Try and follow if you dare.

On Hallowe'en it is cool,
I will dress up like a ghoul,
I think the Devil
Is very evil.
I know a skeleton,
Do not run, it's just her son.

Hallowe'en is when spirits come alive,
Then they thrive,
Hallowe'en is when the anger comes out,
Then you run without a doubt,
If you see a ghastly ghoul,
Just be sure to go to school.

On Hallowe'en, pumkins are lit,
Then we tell stories while we sit,
Trick or treaters come for money,
Sometimes scones dripping with honey,
Some of us hang an apple on a tree,
Some of us just watch TV.

Gordon Robertson (9)
Sea View Private School

MILLENNIUM BUG

Power would be no more,
Water would not pour,
Gas would not heat,
How would we cook our meat?
Clocks would not tick
What about the sick?
Would hospitals cope?
What would happen to us folk?

2000 is the year
Which we have learned to fear,
The ministers keep watching,
In case the Bug comes crawling near.
It's 12 o'clock and counting
The fears are now subsiding
The Bug, it has not bitten
The world just goes on turning.

Ewen Cameron
Sea View Private School

SUMMER

Summer is the type of season
I like, there is a reason,
The sun is hot, the days are long,
The children joyfully sing a song.

The girls are skipping,
The boys are kicking,
The ball so high, it reached the sky,
This created a great big sigh.

Tumbling down the colours came,
Oh! To start another game,
Running swiftly just to catch,
The ball again for another match.

Paul Bilan (11)
Sea View Private School

WRESTLING

Wrestling is my favourite thing,
My favourite thing of all,
With De-Generation
As the new leaders,
And my favourite group of all.

To see them battling in the ring,
Makes my heart go faster,
Just wondering who will win,
Each move is hard to master.
That is why,
My favourite guy,
Is the Rattler.

Stone Cold is the best,
The best there ever was,
Stone Cold is the best,
The best there ever will be,
Stone Cold is the champion
And he always will be.

Blaine Young (10)
Sea View Private School

MARS

Mars is big and round,
Mars is big, round and red,
You see it at night-time,
Just before you go to bed.

Mars is named after a messenger,
Who delivered good news most of the time.
He ran through the town with a bell,
Ringing the bell to make it chime.

Mars is hot in the morning,
And very cold at night,
If you look up at the sky tonight,
It is going to shine very bright.

Mars had running water once,
Just like we do,
But poor old Mars,
He died of the flu.

Christopher Coyne (10)
Sea View Private School

RACE CARS

Race cars are fast,
Not wanting to come last,
They go down the track,
Never looking back.

Their wheels are round
They speed across the ground,
If you break your seat
That's no reason to cheat.

The race cars can really fly,
And the birds will fly in the sky,
But if you win, lose or draw
Come out with your head up high.

Jamie Caira (10)
Sea View Private School

THUNDERSTORM

Thunder echoes all around
Stormy weather keeps boats aground
People up and people down
They don't look, they just turn around

Thunder echoes all around
Now and then I hear the sound
Everyone's scared all but me
Why do they just look and see?

William Proudfoot (10)
Strathmiglo Primary School

CHEETAHS

C reeping quietly without a sound
H eart beating ready to pounce
E yes fixed like the moon to the Earth
E ventually jumps and grabs for his meal
T he antelope runs, gasping for air
A nother good catch as good as having
   a million-pound spare
H ome she comes with a fill for her cubs
S leeping quietly in her den at last.

Ronan Fraser (10)
Strathmiglo Primary School

FOOTBALL

F lying ball as fast as lightning
O ver all the people
O n it goes and into the goal
T oo fast for the goalkeeper
B illy is Goalie
A nd I am striker
L onely goes the floating ball
L osing team is going home.

Scott Eadie (10)
Strathmiglo Primary School

SPRINT

S uper-fast like a jet
P eople come to make a bet
R ugy players come to see how super-fast
I can be
N ow I am a super winner
T hough I had to eat my dinner.

Billy Robertson (10)
Strathmiglo Primary School

FOOTBALL

F lying down the wing as fast as lightning
O ut and in all the players
O ver all the tacklers
T ime ticks away as fast as sound just about
B eing tackled, crosses the ball in for a head
A nd that's it, goal! Must be the winner 1-0
L ike a flash they celebrate
L osing team leave in shame.

Grant Thomas (9)
Strathmiglo Primary School

RACE AROUND BRITAIN

R ound the world in a hot air balloon
A berdeen, the lights as bright as fire
C oming on now to bonnie Edinburgh
E dinburgh is very cold if you go to the Castle

A t 1 o'clock you will hear a loud bang
R ound the corner we have *huge* Glasgow
O n some nights, bands play at the SECC
U nder a *huge* roof
N o more time in Glasgow, let's move on to Dundee
D undee has a brill pool with flumes.

B ig as skyscrapers in New York
R ound the corner to Cupar
I t's got a great ice-cream shop, let's move on
T o the great Aberdour
A berdour has a brilliant beach and baker's
I n and out of these places
N ow it's time to go. Hope you enjoyed your *tour!*

Laura Farrington (10)
Strathmiglo Primary School

SWEETS

S weets, red as red as a tomato,
W e all like Skittles, Aeros and Minstrels,
E ating them makes us sick,
E verything is getting clean, as clean
   as we first got it,
T oday I will be off school,
S o better go to bed,
                    goodnight!

Claire Lunardi (10)
Strathmiglo Primary School

BEDTIME

'B edtime,' says Mum and Dad
'E nd of the day,' says my best granny
D ark the night, as black as the witch
T ime for stories of friendly giants
I n the morning comes the sun, so go to sleep
M um comes up and tucks me in
E normous Dream Giant says *Goodnight!*

Lorraine Gordon (10)
Strathmiglo Primary School

VALENTINE

V alentine's Day is lots of fun, getting cards from your mystery one.
A ll of the cards and all of the things, you will be receiving
from the one you love.
L ove as sweet as kisses
E very one is precious
N othing like the touch of your lips
T ogether as forever
I n Heaven love is sweet
N othing else does matter
E ternity is forever in this heaven of love.

Eternity!

Judith Keiller (9)
Strathmiglo Primary School

Sea Storm At Night

S ea storm starts
E asily the waves slice the shore apart
A ll the small rocks are swept away as easily as pulling
   a pencil along a table
S ea rises into the sky
T iny stones are swept ashore
O ver all the sand as cold as ice
R ocks all disappear beneath the waves
M eters high, the waves collide with the shore
A s cold as the Arctic, nothing's left dry
T oo much water no more
N ow more, more, more and still more waves
I n and out tidal waves as tall as skyscrapers
G igantic waves are dying down
H ow much more water to go?
T he waves have died down and the tide is going out

Conor Smart (9)
Strathmiglo Primary School

BIRDS

B irds are many shapes and sizes

I in and out they swoop

R ight and left in many ways

D oing things you would have thought

S inging beautifully like a flute.

Alice Cook (9)
Strathmiglo Primary School

SUNNY DAY

S unny day on the beach
U mbrella in a cupboard until winter
N eeding buckets and spades to play in the sand
N othing to worry us today
Y ou need an ice-cream in the sun

D o you know when we're to go for tea?
A nd then we went home
Y um, yum, tea is ready at last.

Nadine Bruce (10)
Strathmiglo Primary School

THE SAILOR MAN

On a sunny day
The sailor looked across the bay
It was a lovely day
The sky was blue
The poor old sailor had a touch of flu.
He took a swig of rum
Then fell and broke his thumb
He let out a yell
Hit his head on the bell.
He slipped over a rope
And lost all hope.
He thought he was dead
But he'd landed in bed
The best place he could be
There he decided to stay
And not look out over the bay.

Dean Dorans (8)
Tanshall Primary School

TELEVISION

I like to watch television
It makes me giggle and laugh
But half way through the best bits
I get sent for a bath.
My favourite is Ground Force
Their gardens are a wreck
But when my dad comes home from work
He flicks it to Star Trek.
I am only little can't you see
And only try my best
So Mum and Dad please, please, please!
Let me watch the rest!

Kirsty McLeod (9)
Tanshall Primary School

WORLD WAR I

Very few survived
So very few alive
Many injured or killed
And we ask ourselves why?
Did so many die
Survivors fought in Flanders Fields for King and country.
Would we be here if we lost the war?
I think not somehow.
Women weep as husbands, sons and fathers go to war.
Most of the war was not fought in the air or the sea.
But in Flanders Fields so far away.
Guns, canons and other weapons fell silent.
On the 11th day of the 11th month of the 11th hour in 1918.
Armistice Day is when I believe the first snowflake fell
and a treaty was signed.
Poppies now grow in Flanders Fields
A symbol of blood that will forever grow
in Flanders Fields.

Claire Aitken (11)
Tanshall Primary School

My Dream

There's something going on outside
I don't know what it is,
I hear the wind and rain
I think I'm going insane,
Mum says 'Don't be silly
and go back to bed,'
I run through the hall
Jump in my bed,
I hear howling winds
but I try to go to sleep.
I wake up
The sun is shining,
I say to myself,
'It was all a dream.'

Kimberley Giles (9)
Tanshall Primary School

STARS

I see a star up in the sky
I wonder why they are up so high
Maybe if they got too close
They would turn us all to toast.
Stars are in a cluster
They look so bright
Twinkling and reflecting in the darkness of the night.
As the light comes towards the earth
And disappear as new ones birth.

Stacy Raker (12)
Tanshall Primary School

THE WAY I FEEL

Today I feel sad
Things are real bad.
It makes me mad
When I fall out with my dad.

Now I sit at school alone
Wishing I was still at home.
Listening to others moan
But I just nod and give a groan.

Sitting at school I can't wait to get out
On the way home they shove and shout.
I felt like giving one of them a bout
But I don't want to be a lout.

I feel like I have been separated from the class
Then they came around the corner in a mass.
I feel like a mouse trapped in a glass
I hide round a corner till they pass.

Allan Mill (12)
Tayport Primary School

MY SISTER!

My sister is moany,
I think it's her age,
She's always blaming me for things,
She should be in a cage.

She's always going out with friends
And never plays with me,
When coming in from her papers
And shouting 'What's for tea?'

When she's in her room,
I knock on her door and she shouts 'What?'
I say 'Can I come in?'
And she shouts back 'Not.'

She absolutely worships Westlife,
But I think they're abominable,
Posters all over the place,
It's totally horrible.

She's always on the playstation
And never gives me a shot,
She makes my tea all soggy,
When she cooks it in the pot.

My sister says I'm annoying,
But she's really the pain,
We fight every minute of the day,
But I love her all the same.

Lorna Gray (11)
Tayport Primary School

SPORT

Sport is something I love to do,
I really like football and tennis too!
Sports are great I love them all
I've thought they were great since I was small.

Riding my bike is always fun,
I sometimes go for a cycle run.
Golf is a nice, relaxing sport,
Where it's go, go, go on the tennis court.

Horse riding is what my friends like to do,
With horses called Lady and Caspian too.
I prefer football to a horse's stable,
I'm always out playing it when my tea's on the table.

I really like to play basketball,
But no, wait, that's not all,
Table tennis is OK
But I never really get a chance to play.

I think I like tennis the best
But oh no what about the rest,
Or maybe it's football;
Who really cares, I love them all.

Andrew Reid (11)
Tayport Primary School

POOR PEOPLE

Here's a story that I don't really want to tell
How many people in many places have to sell, sell, sell!
They sell for their family
They sell for their food
They would sell to anyone
If they possibly could.

Children are frightened
They don't know when
Their meals are going to come
They have to go a long way to have fun, fun, fun!

While we are cosy in our houses,
Drinking hot chocolate
Just think some people don't even have blouses.
We are very lucky people,
Just think about people far away,
They have nowhere to go or nowhere to stay!

Coral Robertson (11)
Tayport Primary School

GOLF

Arrival time is here at last
I asked my Mum to go more fast
We walk out onto the first tee
All eyes were set then on me.

I hope to hit the ball straight
As it goes in hole number eight
I managed to get a hole in one
Even though my fingers were numb.

Onto hole number ten
I write my scores with a pen
To my opponent I said 'Good hit'
He said 'I hope you die in the pit.'

I tee off
Oh I love this game of golf
I hope to play it all my life
With my skills as sharp as a knife.

Paul Martin (11)
Tayport Primary School

COMPANIONS

Friends are loads of fun
It's great to have super chums
They listen to your secrets
And won't tell anyone.

They help you with your homework
When you are really stuck
But if the teacher found out that
I think she'd run amuck!

They're great to go out shopping with
They give you good advice
But there's one bad thing about them
They are never there on time!

They are loyal and they are kind
They are always in my mind
I don't think you could ever find
Anything quite like them!

Laura Redpath (11)
Tayport Primary School

MY FRIENDS

My best friend is Laura
She is a shopaholic
She likes to go to discos
Where we laugh and frolic.

Cheryl is another friend
She is absolutely mad
She loves to watch the wrestling
And chat with all the lads.

Lorna is a funny friend
She is pretty crazy
When she's not inventing stuff
She's probably talking to Maisie.

Jenny is my soul mate
Dancing is her passion
She's always at it everywhere
She is also into fashion.

Shannon is a shy friend
She is really very horse mad
She talks about them all the time
And she's never, ever bad.

So they are all my ace chums
They really are lots of fun
They're very kind to their mums
They are the best friends under the sun!

Nicola Whatley (11)
Tayport Primary School

WASPS

I hate summer
The wasps are out
Those little dark and scary things
Flying in the air
But when you annoy them
You're in for a shock!

I'm allergic to wasps
When they sting me my arm inflames
If they do I have to go to the doctors
I get cream to put on every day.

My brother just laughs
When I cry
My sister laughs as well
I hate summer
The wasps are out that's why.

Laura Towns (11)
Tayport Primary School

GOLF

It's 7 o'clock in the morning,
On the first tee,
Waiting until it's my turn,
To hit the ball on a run.

You have to use a golf club,
To hit the ball far,
Even though I can't get a par,
I am not doing very well so far.

You're not allowed to wear sports clothes,
So you have to wear golf clothes,
Even though I can hardly go,
I like to hit the golf ball low.

I'm on the eighteenth tee,
My Dad waiting for me,
I hit the ball on the green
And my partner hits it in the rough
And I say that's rather tough.

Bradley Burnett (11)
Tayport Primary School

FRIENDS!

Jenna is my bestest friend
She loves to go shopping
She runs about with all the boys
And leaves her friends hopping!

Zarra and Shannon are my funny friends
They like to go very mad,
They chat a lot about their mates
But also about the *lovely* lads!

Ruth is my wild friend
She likes to wrestle and sing
And when it's time for her to fight
She's first into the ring!

Andrew is my daring friend
His favourite sport is tennis,
He is always getting into trouble
And to me he's just a menace.

Matthew is my mad friend
He tries to impress us lasses,
He's mostly boring after school
But not in his classes.

Stacey Mullen (11)
Tayport Primary School

I DON'T LIKE MY BROTHER

I don't like my brother,
  He doesn't like me,
We are forever fighting,
  He puts me off my tea.

I don't like my brother,
  He makes me very mad,
He sometimes can be good,
  But he can be very bad.

I don't like my brother,
  He drives me round the bend,
He always pulls my hair,
  He'll never be my friend.

I don't like my brother,
  He always calls me names,
He always takes my things as well,
  Especially my games.

I don't like my brother,
  He annoys me night and day,
He never stops moaning,
  But I suppose he is okay!

Zarra Swan (11)
Tayport Primary School

SQUIRRELS

Running up the tree trunk
Dashing tree to tree
Collecting nuts for winter days
Dashing back to sleep.

Their thick, fuzzy, bushy tails
Their small, furry bodies
Must keep them warm
In winter weather.

Their colours are bright and full
Greyish and reddish such peculiar colours
Their eyes are gleaming black
You cannot see them in the dark.

What they collect are different nuts
Chestnuts and walnuts, acorns too
Crunching, munching at their nuts
Or storing away for winter weather.

Paula Hughes (11)
Tayport Primary School

My Dog

My big, fluffy dog
Always chasing other dogs
Here one minute, gone the next
Never knowing when he'll be back.

My dog is very playful
Never being careful
His big paws skidding everywhere
Messing up his fluffy hair.

His white and orange hair
He's like a big, furry bear
But maybe not as scary
But certainly as hairy.

He likes to chase cats
In and out of the flats
But he's always home for dinner
Never getting any thinner.

Ruth Barnett (11)
Tayport Primary School

FOOTBALL

Football, football a game of two halves
If you score a goal
It brings lots of laughs
Even if it's a muck about, it's still just great.

Waiting in the dressing room before the match,
Adrenaline pumping, no turning back.
In formation before the whistle,
Then it goes, it's started, let's go.

The supporters roar like lions, hungry for their food
Then a goal is scored,
They roar even more,
Ten minutes to half-time, hold on till then!

All at once another goal is scored,
Oh no the other supporters roar,
Two minutes to go until you can relax,
A sending off 'Boo' the crowd shout.

In the second half, the crowd are roaring,
This is really boring,
Five minutes to go, a penalty is won,
Nice one, my son.

Scott Crosby Reid (11)
Tayport Primary School

FRIENDS

There for you when you need them,
Always at your side,
Helpful with your homework,
But never there on time.

Help each other get ready,
For going to Dundee,
Mum can I have some money
Please? I'm in a hurry.

Friends are helpful,
Loving and kind,
With a very
Funny mind.

They keep you company when you're down
And have fun when you're around.
Stay overnight at each other's house,
Stay up late till there is no sound.

There for you when you need them,
Always at your side,
Helpful with your homework,
But never there on time!

Rebecca White (11)
Tayport Primary School

FRIENDS

My friends are very kind
With a lot of mad minds
They are caring
And very daring
They are also very helpful
Sometimes they can be peaceful!

My friends are always there
They seem to pop up everywhere
If you've got a problem
They'll help you sort it out
If somebody hurts you
They'll give them a clout.

Jenna
Jenna is never sad
She is always very mad
She is always game for a laugh
Falling about on the grass
She always wears coloured socks
And hates going for long walks.

Rebecca
Rebecca is a sensible friend
She always has letters to send
She's not mad like Jenna
But sometimes she can be a blether
We like to go to Dundee
Just Rebecca and me.

Kimberley Clark (11)
Tayport Primary School

FOOTBALL

Getting ready to go to training
Even though it's absolutely raining.
Cold and getting muddy
Even though it is a bit funny.

The next day you're getting ready to play
It's never, ever a bonnie day.
Kicking and tackling for the ball
I'd rather be kicking it at the wall.

Even though we usually get beat
At least try to play like Emanuel Petit.
When I'm kicking the ball with my friends
I'd think we'd rather be at Den's.

I like playing in the goals
At least I get some help from metal poles.
Trying to save the ball with my gloves
While telling my brother not to shove.

Steven Grogan (11)
Tayport Primary School

TITCH

I have a puppy his name is Titch
On his nose he has a bad itch.
He likes to come with me when I go to my bed
And always looks up at me with his cute, little head.

He likes to play with my dad's sock
And also likes to go on a long walk.
He piddles at the front door
But he never is a bore.

Titch really likes liver cake
But it takes a long time for me to make.
He loves it when I let him off the lead
So that he can have a good feed.

Titch is a Yorkshire Terrier
Every day he gets merrier.
His colour is blue and tan
If he was any smaller, he would fit in a can.

I love my puppy Titch
Even though he has a bad itch.
Titch has got a squint tail
I still love my other dog too
Even though he is a bit frail.

Shannon Moncur (11)
Tayport Primary School

WAKING UP

Beep, beep, beep, beep.
It's early hours of the morning
as my eyes are sluggishly adjusting to the dark,
opening to the glowing digits of my little, white alarm clock.

I give a tiny yawn, roll over on my side
and feel for a little black button go click,
I then with a sigh of relief, snuggle back into my warm duvet
and imagine the time has stopped.
Both night and day.

I then hear my door and suddenly stare at the floor
as I wait for familiar feet.
The bare feet of my mum, oh no here they come.
They meet the side of my double bed
and then they suddenly stop.
Closely followed with the dreaded words
'Come on sleepy head, hop out of bed!'
They echo around in my head.

I reluctantly step out of bed
feeling the warmth that's left behind,
and shiver as the coldness runs down my spine.
I then think to myself as I begin to get dressed
oh well I've had my rest
and dread the morning to come!

Lauren McGivney (12)
Tayport Primary School

LION

A big, fluffy mane,
With large, sharp jaws,
Two big, beady eyes
And a wet, jet nose.

Huge, round paws,
With sharp, pointed claws,
A long, furry tail
And a tremendous appetite.

When his tummy rumbles
He gets really hungry.
Now he stands up
And observes his prey.

His prey is eating grass,
While he is running fast,
Scaring them to death
By being very aggressive.

Catching a little one
And ripping it apart,
The blood flying everywhere
And breaking the mother's heart.

When he has finished,
The hyenas come to eat,
He lies back in the shade
And goes back to sleep.

Rachel Hutchison (11)
Tayport Primary School

PLOUGHING

The horse slowly wobbling up and down the fields all day,
Shaking with exhaustion in the cold air.
The sound of its hooves squelching in the soft mud,
Puffing and panting and making all kinds of noises,
Swishing its long, white tail.
Turning the wet, clammy grass,
Scraping on little stones,
Forcing them out in all directions . . .

Nicola Gourlay (11)
Thornton Primary School

THE PLOUGHMAN

The cow plodding on snorting, rolling.
Rubbing muscles, aches and pains,
Tightening skin over the body,
Grinding bones, stumbling,
The horse's feet are like four rocks.
They lift up then smash into the mud.
The muscles in the rump rolling from side to side,
The sleek metal shining off the sunrise.
The plough blade slicing a clean cut
Through the viscous mud.
Splintering wood handles,
Sweaty leather reins tightening around
The ploughboy's hands,
Pain stretching across his shoulders.
Ankles are aching, toes are blistering
Hot, steaming leather boots
Going home soon!

Matthew Low (11)
Thornton Primary School

I WOULD LIKE TO

I would like to feel the colourful
Magic of the dreamy sunset and
Drag the colours of the sun like wet
Paint on the paper.

I would like to smell the sweaty, jagged
Spikes on the cat's back and the
Shuddering odour of the cat's fear in the light
Of the cat's green, cold eyes.

I would like to touch the smooth
Silky water and feel the rushing of people
Swimming past in a blur of colour.

I would like to smell the damp dew on the
Grass in the morning.

Daniel Robinson (11)
Thornton Primary School

I WOULD LIKE TO

I would like to hear the scream of the fear of falling
And feel the resistance of the whooshing wind.

I would like to feel the pattering of rain on the outside of my window
From the warmth of my bedroom.

I would like to see the
Invisible velvet of rippling water
Flowing through my fingers.

Stephanie Clark (11)
Thornton Primary School

ON A BEACH IN OMAN

I would like to feel the smoothness of
Wet paint
Sail across the dreamy sky.

I would like to taste the warm, refreshing air
Trickle down my throat
Like a therapeutic tea.

I would like to feel the effervescence
As the waves bubble in my mouth.

Toni Shaw (11)
Thornton Primary School

PAINTING ON THE CANVAS OF DREAMS

I would like to feel the rushing magic of a
Jurassic waterfall.

I would like to feel the piercing wind as
I run through the towering trees
Of a prehistoric landscape.

I would like to taste the clammy fear
As I stand frigid
On a swinging rope bridge,
Over a gorge
Filled with magic.

I would like to taste the movements of
The dark and eerie river
As it flows mysteriously through
The everlasting blackness.

I would like to smell the darkness
As the canopy of destiny
Closes in
And traps out the daylight
Forever.

I would like to hear the mystical dreams
Calling out for me
As I fill with sadness
And my fantasy is gone.

Andrew Dott (11)
Thornton Primary School

THE PLOUGHBOY POET

The plough slashing beneath the grass with its sharp blades.
The grass swirling in the twisting, turning whirlwind.
The man feeling hot and bothered,
Sweating from head down,
Dragging his dirty sleeve across his brow.
Heavy feet clunking down on the hard soil.
Raw bunions sticking out of his toes,
Rubbing onto his harsh leather boots.
His arms strong, rough, pushing the swerving plough.
Guiding it through the dry slime.

Lyndsay McLaren (11)
Thornton Primary School